MW01679525

time with your King

Interactive Journal

DECHARI COLE

Time With Your King *(Interactive Journal)* copyright © 2021 by Dechari Cole. All rights reserved.

Unless otherwise noted, all Scripture is from the Scripture quotations marked (HCSB) are taken from the Holman Christian Standard Bible®, Copyright © 1999, 2000, 2002, 2003 by Holman Bible Publishers. Used by permission. Holman Christian Standard Bible®, Holman CSB®, and HCSB® are federally registered trademarks of Holman Bible Publishers.

Scripture quotations marked ESV are from the ESV® Bible (The Holy Bible, English Standard Version®), copyright © 2001 by Crossway Bibles, a publishing ministry of Good News Publishers. Used by permission. All rights reserved.

ISBN Print: 978-1-7359110-2-1

Published by Girls Living 4 God

Printed in the United States of America

Book Cover + Interior Book Design Layout by
Sarah O'Neal | *eve custom artwork*

GL4G
GIRLS LIVING 4 GOD

For More Information and to purchase the book
please visit GirlsLiving4God.com

Dearest Daughter of the Most High,

God your father and King has so much He wants to impart to you! As you spend time with Him, the depths of His love will overflow - bringing freedom, strength, wisdom, joy and purpose in your life.

Take hold of this time to grow and truly embrace your identity as His beautiful, beloved, chosen daughter and heir.

Be on guard as you start this journey. The enemy will try to deceive you of its importance and steal your time with distractions!

Spending time with your King will be the most valuable and life-giving part of your day!

HOW TO USE

Community

Journeys are best traveled with friends! Prayerfully invite people to commit to going through Finding Your Fairy Tale Ending with you. Gather weekly to encourage and sharpen one another in the faith as you seek God together.

Soak on Scripture

We've included beautiful scripture pages to color and make your own. Take this time to dwell on the truth and love your King extends to you.

Reflection Questions

We've given you questions based on each chapter to go deeper in both group discussion and personal reflection. This is where you can seek God and His Word for wisdom and truth.

Journaling

We've included plenty of room to journal through this journey. Grab your favorite pens and stickers and get creative as you write what God is teaching you!

Heart To Heart

We've provided some conversation starters to help you pour out your heart to God. Prompted by Jesus' prayer in Matthew 6:8-13, we want you to remember who God is, give thanks, share your heart and needs, and take any sin hindering you to your forgiving Father.

Your Takeaway

You'll find a beautiful open page for your biggest takeaways. Whether you draw or write, let this be a special place to remember Whose you are and that He loves you.

Expectations

Expect God to speak to you! He wants you to know His voice and His Word! Pray before each lesson and ask Him to grow you during this time. Journal those whispers to your heart and where you see God at work.

CONTENTS

time with your King

He alone is my rock & my salvation my STRONGHOLD; I will not be shaken.

psalms 62:6

chapter 1 Reflection

1. Jesus says that God's Word is our only true foundation for life, and Matthew 7 talks at length about how we should live. Read all of Matthew 7 for yourself. What foundation principles for your life can you find?

2. When something tough comes crashing down on you, where do you run for strength? Have you ever run from God? Sometimes it seems that when you need someone the most, no one is around. Might that be because God wants you to run to Him?

3. Read Romans 8:28 and 1 Peter 1:6-7. Can you think of an experience in your life that seemed negative at first but later turned out for good? Did you become stronger for it? What are some biblical examples of this?

4. How can your struggles affect your relationship with God? Do you think your trials can be used to bring glory to God and to point others to Him?

5. Though you may not be going through an immediate crisis, do you know someone who is? Can you lift him or her up in prayer? What other ways can you be supportive? Be specific!

Take this opportunity to share some of your story (the good and the bad) with those taking this journey with you. Trust that the Lord is writing your story so that the world will know Him!

heart to heart

Jesus, be my Rock!

I struggle with building my life and worth on the shifting foundations of...

Instead, help me to trust...

Bring good out of...

Please forgive me for running to...

Thank You that You've got me and I can always run to You no matter what storms come.

I am his

he is mine

YOU WILL

seek me

& find me

WHEN

you search for me with

all your heart

jeremiah 29:13

a little heart to heart

1. Read Matthew 5:20-28. Let this be eye-opening and humble us to not think of ourselves more highly than we should (Romans 12:3) but bring us back to the fact that we all have sinned (Romans 3:23) and all need the grace of Jesus (Romans 5:8)!

2. Have you been living in **pride** *("At least I haven't done the things she's done")* or **shame** *("I will never be as good as her or loved like her")*? Will you bring that to Jesus today and let Him nail it to the cross? What do you think would happen if we stop judging our sisters and instead straighten their crown and remind them who they are in Jesus?

3. What was *your* previous definition of "purity"? How has that changed, or has it? Is purity available to everyone through Jesus?

4. Jesus hasn't called us to perfection but called us to love! Read 1 John 4:16-21. Knowing and believing *(abiding)* in His love for us changes how we live. It enables us to love others! In this, love is being perfected in us. But what do you think happens if we start striving for perfection to "earn" His love and just follow all the rules instead of accepting that His love was already freely given?

Jesus, You know my heart!

Help my heart to…

Heal the part of my heart that…

Thank You for…

I give You my…

Let me rest in knowing I am already loved by You completely as I am right now. Instead of me working just to follow all the rules, let me follow You. Work on my heart to show me more of You and Your love and plan for me!

I am his

he is mine

He will give you another HELPER to be with you forever

John 14:16 ESV

chapter 2

Reflection

1. High School was a new adventure for me. A lot of emotions can accompany new beginnings. Is there something new you are entering into? How do you feel about it? How are you inviting God into this new thing?

2. Check out these verses about the Holy Spirit: Romans 8:26–27, Galatians 5:16–25, John 14:15–18, Acts 4:31, and 1 Corinthians 2:10–16. Who is the Holy Spirit and what does He do? Can you find other verses that mention the Holy Spirit?

3. "Remember, God gives us the Holy Spirit to help us discern things." What does discernment mean? Have you seen specific examples when God has given you discernment to say no, to avoid or leave a place or situation, etc.?

4. Are there people in your life that often persuade you to think/do/say things that aren't in line with what Jesus would want? Read Proverbs 13:20. Saying no can be difficult, but the Holy Spirit can help you. If you need to distance yourself from a toxic relationship, will you start praying with a parent, trusted Godly friend or mentor who can help keep you accountable?

5. Daughter of God, I want you to hear that you are priceless and to be treasured and respected! Have you ever had someone try to guilt you into doing something you didn't want to do or felt violated? It's not okay and not your fault. What did Joseph do in Genesis 39:6-12? Where can we run for help? Don't keep this to yourself. Tell a parent, counselor, mentor or church leader who can help.

heart to heart

God, You have sent me the Helper, the Holy Spirit!

Thank You…

Lead me in these decisions of…

Protect me from…

Forgive me for…

Help me walk with You, God, by inviting You into my decisions and asking for the Holy Spirit's guidance. Let me lean on the Holy Spirit to teach me Your Word and Your heart,

I am his

he is mine

blessed
are those who
DWELL
in your house
ever
singing
your
praise.

psalm 84:4 esv

chapter 3 Reflection

1. Nehemiah 8:10 tells us that our strength is in the joy of the Lord. Spending time worshiping God and having good, clean fun with other Christians filled my spirit and got me through the week with joy. Have you learned to have fun with God? How so, or why not?

2. Read Ephesians 4:9-10 and Proverbs 27:17. What does your support group look like? Do your friends sharpen you (make you a better person) and bring you closer to God? How can you start sharpening others in their faith?

3. Read Hebrews 10:24-25. We are created for community! The church is an important place for those who love Jesus to worship God *together*, gain instruction on how to live for God and lift one another up. Have you invested your time into a local church? Have you just been checking it off as a to-do, or are you asking God, "What is my role in the church?"

4. You share with your friends when you have good news, right? So why do you think people are so hesitant to share the Good News of Jesus? Discuss what obstacles you've encountered and what has helped you. How can you and your friends sharpen one another to grow in this area?

5. Read Romans 10:14-15. Pray that God will open up opportunities for you to share Him with others. Who is one person you want to start praying for? Write down their name. Sharing can be as easy as telling them about the great things God has done for you and how He has comforted you in hard times. Ask the Holy Spirit to help!

heart to heart

Jesus, You are my joy
and strength!

I praise You for…

Forgive me …

Sharpen me to…

Help me share the good news of Jesus with...

God, You alone refresh my soul like nothing else! Let Your praises be on my lips, and let my paths be paved with the good news of Jesus wherever I am that others may know You.

I am his

he is mine

Charm is deceptive & beauty is fleeting but a woman who fears the Lord will be PRAISED.

PROVERBS 31:30

chapter 4

Reflection

1. If you are currently in a relationship, what is keeping you in it? Is it just physical attraction? The attention? How can you make sure it's not superficial? Read 1 Corinthians 13:4-8 and list the true definition of what love looks like.

2. What's a healthy approach in getting to know someone that won't result in a broken heart or regret if it doesn't work out?

3. Read 1 Samuel 16:6-13. Never count someone out - including yourself - when it comes to who God uses. God uses the unlikely to do the impossible! Have you ever discounted yourself or others based on physical limitations or appearances? What are your limitations with God? Read Luke 1:37.

4. Speaking generally (not just romantically), do you feel that you give people a chance? Do you try to get to know them no matter their appearance? Are there people who have surprised you once you got to know them–both good and bad?

5. Look at Proverbs 31:30 again. Are you more than your appearance? Of course, you are! How can you grow your inner beauty?

heart to heart

God, You are the One who sees my heart!

Nothing is impossible for You, not even...

Thank You for...

Help me ...

Forgive me...

God, I pray that I too learn to look deeper at those around me and see them how You do. God, take me past the superficial things I'm tempted to put value in and create in me a beautiful heart! (Psalm 51:10)

I am his

he is mine

whatever
YOU do,
do it
enthusiastically
as something
DONE
for the
LORD.

Colossians 3:23

chapter 5 Reflection

1. What would starting your day talking to God look like? What difference do you see in your mood and how you react to things after you've spent time with God versus those days you hurry on without Him?

2. Do you realize that **joy** is a tremendous gift that is available to all believers of Jesus no matter your circumstance? We can choose joy! It is actually a *fruit*, a result, of the Holy Spirit in our lives (Galatians 5:22). Read James 1:2-8 and Colossians 1:9-13. Could asking God for wisdom in our lives help us to have joy? How so? Do you see any previous lessons we've discussed in the Colossians 1 passage?

3. Read Acts 16:22-34. Choosing joy can look like praising God, even in the midst of our hardest battles. How does doing this change us and the people around us?

4. If you start living knowing Jesus can use you wherever you are, how does that change your ultimate purpose and attitude at that job, in that group, on that team, in your class, etc.? Do you believe God can use you in whatever you do?

5. What do you think is the difference in God's joy and the world's definition of happiness?

6. Read 1 Timothy 4:12. Be an example in your youth! My actions showed I could be trusted as I was responsible for more things. List qualities you want to be known for.

heart to heart

God, You give me joy!

Thank You...

Will You help me have joy...

Forgive me for...

God, You are...

I am so grateful that my joy and strength don't come from my circumstances, but from You and Your Holy Spirit. I pray my joy is full as I focus on shining You wherever I am. ☺

I am his

he is mine

STAY AWAKE

& PRAY so that YOU WON'T enter into temptation.

Matthew 26:41

chapter 6

Reflection

1. What do you think about the way I changed some of my habits because I was trying to impress the guy I was dating? Do you change how you act depending on who you are around? What about how you act at church versus school versus social media? Why do we struggle with being authentic?

2. Read 2 Timothy 2:22. What is lust? We talked about love's definition (1 Corinthians 13:4-8) previously in Chapter 4. I said I shouldn't have been as passionate (physical) with my boyfriend. So how do we run from lust and run towards love in our life and relationships?

3. What boundaries (guardrails to keep you away from the edge) can you set up to help with this pursuit of love and not lust?

4. Do you feel guilt for the things you struggle with? Guess what! Jesus isn't out to shame you (condemnation) but to set you free to turn from sin (conviction). Read John 3:16-17 and 1 John 1:7–9. How does this make you feel? What is the difference between condemnation (that is Satan's voice) and conviction (that is the Holy Spirit's voice)? How might recognizing these two voices help set you free?

5. We are all tempted by things in this world, whether that's sexual immorality, lust, pornography, explicit novels, etc. Maybe it's something else you may or may not realize is destructive like gossip, self-harm, pride, perfectionism, alcohol or drugs. 1 Corinthians 10:12-13 says God makes a way out of temptation. Let's create an "escape plan" with the Lord and one another so we can stay away from that ledge!
   - » Start with these scriptures: 1 Peter 5:8-9 · Ephesians 6:10-18 · Galatians 6:1-2 Psalm 119:105 · James 1:5 · Galatians 5:22-25

heart to heart

God, You are the definition of love!

Help me to understand...

Thank You for...

Forgive me for....

God, as I seek out love, let me receive Your love first! Teach me how to love and be loved and not settle for lust. Protect my heart and mind as I grow in wisdom.

I am his

he is mine

Why do you LOOK at the speck in your brother's eye but DON'T notice the Log in your OWN eye?

MATTHEW 7:3

chapter

7 Reflection

1. Read Matthew 7:1-3. We are naturally quick to judge, but we are not so innocent. Why can we so easily point out someone else's flaws yet glance over our own sin? So how can we do heart-checks in this area of judging?

2. When was the last time you sat down with God and asked Him to reveal something He needs to clean up in your own heart? Read Psalm 51:1-10.

3. What do you remember from our previous *"Little Heart to Heart"* conversation? Why should we extend grace and not shame others?

4. Why do you think I wanted a boyfriend so badly after breaking up with Coleson? Why do you think girls want a "boyfriend" sometimes instead of a "boy friend?" What does this label really mean for your relationship?

5. If flirting and dating is a game, then someone loses. Too often we have little regard for the magnitude of the impact we are making on someone's heart and emotions. Read Proverbs 4:23 and Philippians 4:6-7. How can you not only think about guarding your heart but think about these guys' hearts as well? What could this look like?

heart to heart

Jesus, thank You that instead of judging me, You died for me!

Help me not to judge...

I want to pray for...

Show me...

Forgive me for...

God, You have forgiven me so much. Let me be quick to show grace instead of judgment. Let me pray for them and point them to Jesus because of how I love.

I am his

he is mine

1 John 1:7

if we walk in the Light as HE himself is in the LIGHT, we have FELLOWSHIP with one another.

chapter 8 Reflection

1. Friendships take effort. In today's world, we try to have as many "friends" that follow us on social media, but take a look at Proverbs 18:24. Who are your true friends that stand by you and lift you up? What friend qualities do you want to have? Do you need to ask God for this friend who sticks closer than a brother?

2. Savor the moments this year! It will be gone before you know it, and all you'll have left are the memories. Just like my nontraditional prom and Young Life game nights, what are some memories you can make with friends that are "outside the box"? Think scavenger hunts, game nights, craft parties, dinner parties, disco parties, festivals, Christian concerts and events. Be creative! While you're at it, create a *Making Memories Wishlist* that you want to accomplish this year.

3. Do you think hanging out and having fun with other Christians can help your relationship with God? How? Here are some Christian organizations you can join or start at your school:

    » High School: (YL) Young Life • (FCA) Fellowship of Christian athletes • (YFC) Youth for Christ

    » College: Delight Ministries • (CRU) Campus Crusade for Christ • InterVarsity Serve with Young Life

4. Read 1 John 1:6 aloud, and then read verse 7. What are the differences in the two verses? Where are you hanging out; are you in the light or in the dark?

heart to heart

God, help me walk in the light with good friends!

Thank You for...

You are...

I need Your help with...

Please forgive me for...

God, I give You my year! Let me walk through it with You and make sweet memories. Even the tough pathways can lead to blessings because You are with me always. (Psalm 65:11)

I am his

he is mine

GUARD your HEART

above all else
for it is the
the SOURCE of

life.

proverbs 4:23

chapter 9

Reflection

part 1

1. Do you think God is trying to keep something good *from* you or *for* you by saying sex is set apart for marriage? Read John 10:10 and Matthew 7:13-14. What does God want for you when He says wait, and what does Satan want for you when he says don't wait?

2. Read Romans 12:1-2. We can't let Satan's influences in the world teach us about sex because he is out to destroy. We need a *NEW* mindset on sex - one taught by the Creator, God! What new things have you learned about God's design, purpose and the value He's placed on you?

3. How do you view yourself and your worth after this chapter? Why do you or why don't you see yourself as priceless and worth being treasured? If you are not receiving God's love and truth over you, how might that affect your relationships?

4. Since God designed sex to supernaturally bind two people together, never to be separated, then what could the emotional, spiritual, and physical effects of having sex outside of marriage be for you both in the present and in the future?

5. Are you willing to step onto this narrow path to purity starting today by first trusting in God's design and instructions? Why or why not? Talk with your parents and friends about your decision. How can you help one another?

heart to heart

God, You have designed me and my body with so much love and purpose!

Thank You for calling me...

Let me glorify You with ...

I am struggling with...

Help me to start trusting...

God, teach me to accept Your love so that I can reflect Your love. Your Spirit is within me, so let me remember I am a place of worship and be an example of Jesus' love.

I am his

he is mine

THEREFORE,

IF ANYONE IS IN CHRIST,

HE IS A

new creation

OLD THINGS HAVE PASSED AWAY,

AND LOOK, NEW THINGS HAVE COME.

2 CORINTHIANS 5:17

chapter 9

Reflection

part 2

1. Do you ever feel like your sins are worse than someone else's? Read John 8:1–11. Can you see that no one should be throwing stones because we all need Jesus' forgiveness? In what areas do you need to ask Jesus to help you leave the destructive patterns of sin behind and start living the fuller life He has for you?

2. Let's do a heart check. Most of us have struggled with pride or shame and may not realize it. Have you found yourself gossiping or thinking about what someone else has done instead of praying for them or showing them kindness, or have you shied away from things or friends that God wants for you because you feel undeserving?

3. Do you believe you are never too far gone to run back to God? What stories can you think of in the Bible where someone failed yet God still forgave them and used them for the Kingdom? Do you believe He can use you too?

4. Do you see the freedom Jesus invites us into? Do you or someone you know need to receive that beautiful dress of righteousness and start new today? Jesus has given you an invitation to the Kingdom! Read Romans 5:8-11 and Romans 10:9-13. Have you accepted or rejected this invitation?

heart to heart

God, I've fallen short but found grace!

Thank You so much for...

I need to give You my old rags of...

Jesus, I __________ Your invitation. I confess I have sinned. Please forgive me. I believe You died and rose again to conquer death and sin for me. I want You to be my Lord!

Help me walk new in...

Now, God, use my story - the good and the bad - to share the goodness of Your grace. You have invited me into this grace by sending Jesus to conquer sin and death for me. It is Jesus' righteousness that clothes me and makes me clean (Isaiah 61:10).

I am his

he is mine

THE heart is MORE DECEITFUL than anything else & incurable— WHO can understand it?

JEREMIAH 17:9

chapter 10 Reflection

1. Have you ever let the desire for popularity, your people-pleasing tendencies, the desire for the path of least resistance, etc. have too much influence on your decisions? When you feel torn between decisions in your life, what or who do you naturally rely on to figure out which way to go? How reliable is that?

2. It was hard to say no to Evan when he pleaded to get back together. My heart really pulled at me to stay, but wisdom said no way. What are the dangers of "just following your heart" like the world says? What does wisdom say in Proverbs 2?

3. Since Jeremiah 17:9 says you can't trust your heart, how do we navigate and decipher our heart's emotions and choose the right path? Let's go treasure hunting for wisdom in these verses. Write down what you see:
   » Philippians 4:6-7 • James 1:5 • Proverbs 16:1-3 • Psalm 119:105 • Galatians 5:24-25 Ephesians 3:14-21.

4. Do you think I should have stayed Evan's girlfriend to help him work through his struggles? Read 1 Corinthians 15:33 and 2 Corinthians 6:14-15. Are you tying yourself to someone going a different direction than you? What could be the implications of that? Might you be stepping into the place of trying to change them instead of letting God do what only He can do?

heart to heart

God, I want to follow Your path for me!

Teach me...

Help me know what to do with...

You are...

Get me back on the path to...

God, many things try to sway me, but I want to make You King of my heart today and every day. Please remind me to stop and pray and seek Your wisdom to stay on the best path You have for me.

I am his

he is mine

MY WAYS are higher than YOUR WAYS.

Isaiah 55:8-9

chapter 11 Reflection

1. How would you define dating? How does adding this "label" to a relationship change it? What have you seen come from dating - both the good and the bad?

2. Knowing that God's ways and thoughts are higher and outside the box of how the world shows us to pursue love, how can we use examples like Boaz and Ruth, Isaac and Rebekah and Jesus Himself to renew our minds in our pursuit of love? (Isaiah 55:8-9, Romans 12:1-2)

3. Are you known by your great hair, clothes, car, grades, sport you play, club you're in? Boaz referenced Ruth's character above anything else (Ruth 3:10-11). What character qualities do you want to be known for? Share an example where you saw someone's character shine even above their natural beauty.

4. When you have time, read through the book of Ruth. You'll love it! For a time she lost everything, but God provided. Read Philippians 4:19. Do you have faith that God will provide what you need when you need it, bringing Him glory, whether that's provision, a home, family, and companionship?

5. Okay. Quiz time (pg. 66)! Should you date or not date right now?

heart to heart

God, Your ways are higher and better!

You are...

Teach me...

Thank You for...

I need Your wisdom with...

God, I need You to show me Your ways. Quiet the voices that shout at me to do it the world's way. I want better! I want Your best! Help mold my character to love like Christ and trust You with my pursuit of love.

I am his

he is mine

LET YOUR Light shine & GIVE glory to your FATHER in Heaven.

matthew 5:16

chapter 12

Reflection

1. God desires a deeper relationship with you. Read Romans 8:35–39 and Psalm 46:10 (all of 46 if you have time). Could times of loneliness or trials be opportunities to grow closer to Him and shine more brightly than before? Who or what has been standing in your way of a deeper relationship with God?

2. To have that joy that shines from within and allows you to be comfortable in your own skin, you can't find your identity in others, in your appearance, or in your talents, but in how God sees you.
   - Read Psalm 139:13–18, 1 Samuel 16:7, Genesis 1:27, 1 John 3:1, 1 Peter 3:3–4, Ephesians 3:18-19 and 1 Corinthians 3:16–17. What truths do you see, and what lies should you stop believing about yourself?

3. Read 2 Timothy 3:16–17 and Ephesians 6:10-18. God's Word equips us for life and the battle. Have you viewed reading the Bible as more of a checklist to be a "good Christian" or the most powerful tool God gives us to live an abundant life with Him? Where do you want to start in equipping yourself for every good work?

4. It was easy for my teen years to be a consuming and self-focused bubble. Can you pause and think about who you might have ignored lately; a sibling who looks up to you, a neighbor who needs help, your parents who just want to know you are still thankful for them? How do you want to be intentional to reach outside of your bubble to bless some people this month?

5. Where is the Lord molding and shaping you this year? What do you think the Lord has been teaching you?

heart to heart

God, You are molding me into something beautiful!

You are...

Thank You for...

I'm sorry I haven't...

Help me to...

God, You are where my strength and help comes from (Isaiah 41:10). When it seems no one is there, You are. I want to pursue You in your Word and spend time talking to You. Continue to mold me.

I am his

he is mine

come to ME all who are weary + burdened and I will give you rest.

Matthew 11:28

chapter

13 Reflection

1. I needed a break–from boyfriends, from my phone, from social media. It helped me to get in a better place with God and experience His strength, comfort and peace. Pray and ask God to highlight something that has too much pull on you. Make a plan to take a break from it so you can be refreshed, seek God and listen. What friend do you want to help hold you accountable? Then, don't forget to testify to how God uses this time!

2. You set aside intentional time to do things with people you love. Do the same with Jesus! You are building a relationship, not checking off a to-do list. Go for a walk. Lie down in a field and read the Bible. Listen to Christian music. Bake, sing, paint, garden, journal at your favorite coffee shop . . . whatever you find that you love doing while talking to Jesus. What are some "dates with Jesus" you want to try? (Tips on page 78)

3. The devil is cunning and smart in keeping us so distracted and busy that we don't connect well with God. Remember, God hasn't gone anywhere. It's us that move closer or farther away. With that in mind, what is one thing you can start doing to protect your time and grow in relationship with God?

4. Those who obey God are called His friends (John 15:15–16), and we can talk to Him like a friend. He really does hear your prayers (Psalm 34:17). Have you had an honest conversation with God lately? Can you learn to talk to Him like your best friend? Why or why not?

It's okay to laugh at ourselves! Now that I've shared one of my most embarrassing moments, what's one of yours?

to heart heart

Jesus, You carry my burdens!

You are...

Thank You...

Help me to set aside...

I want to...

Jesus, I get so busy I forget to be still and come to You for refreshing and rest. Help me not make our time about checking off a list; instead, I want to have a joy-filled relationship with You where I talk to You about everything.

I am his

he is mine

Humble yourselves BEFORE the Lord & HE will EXALT you!

james 4:10

chapter 14

Reflection

1. Read Philippians 2:3-11. Being humble is not putting ourselves down but lifting others up by valuing them and serving them! How did Jesus give us the ultimate example? Are there people you have been putting down that you could be lifting up?

2. Jealousy comes pretty easy, but it sure doesn't make you any happier. How do you fight it? What's the opposite of being jealous? (**Hint**: Read James 3:13–18 to find out.)

3. Isn't it so cool how God can use a young person, a poor person, a not-so-obviously gifted person? We're all created to make an impact! Read Ephesians 2:10 and Ephesians 3:20. It's never about our being good enough; it's always about God being big enough. Have you ever prayed over your talents, your passions, and the things you own and asked God to use them? What is something that comes to mind?

heart to heart

Wow, God! You can use me no matter what!

God, You are...

Forgive me for...

Help me to ...

Thank You for...

God, don't let me wait until I think I'm old enough, rich enough, talented enough - Just let me be willing to be used by You! Help me to say yes when You call me (Isaiah 6:8).

I am his

he is mine

PAY CAREFUL ATTENTION, then to how you Walk

NOT as unwise people but AS WISE.

Ephesians 5:15-17

chapter 15 Reflection

1. Seth honestly would not have made my list of candidates for someone I would date . . . originally. I think we all tend to make that list of what our dream guy should be like - how tall he should be, his build, his talents, interests and so on. Make your list and have a little fun comparing your list to your friends' lists.

2. Okay. Now circle the things that have to do with his heart or his character as the most important. Oops... do you need to add some important things to the list? Read Ephesians 5:25–28 and discuss the qualities you should seek in a godly husband. Then share your new list with your friends.

3. So what do you think about the things I said about kissing? What things should be driving your relationship?

4. Read Proverbs 1:7-9. Are you asking for wisdom in your decisions and respecting boundaries put in front of you, or are you despising what your parents and others are trying to tell you because you don't want to hear it? What's the value in seeking wise counsel?

heart to heart

God, I need your wisdom!

Bring people into my life who...

Thank you for...

You are...

Help me with...

God, help me get my life in the right order. Show me what's important. Point out anything that is out of place and might lead me the wrong way. Help me seek wise counsel from Your Word and others who love You.

I am his

he is mine

Haven't I commanded you: BE STRONG and courageous.

Do not be AFRAID or DISCOURAGED for the LORD YOUR GOD will be with you wherever you go!

joshua 1:9

chapter

16 Reflection

1. Have you ever had your heart broken like I did, whether by a guy, a friend, or even family? Have you reached out to God to give you strength to forgive and move on? Read Matthew 18:21–22 and Ephesians 4:32. Ask God to help you forgive those who have hurt you.

2. Seth broke my heart, but God never will. My heart is safe with God, and so is yours. Check out His promises in Psalm 73:26 and Psalm 34:18. What do they tell you about how God cares for the brokenhearted?

3. God says we will have to endure trials, but He also gives us hope. Do you trust Him with your future? Take a look at a few of my favorite Bible verses: Proverbs 3:5-6, John 16:33, 2 Corinthians 4:8–18, Jeremiah 29:11, and Romans 8:28. What do these verses say to you about trusting God?

4. Do you believe a broken heart can be God's path to something much greater?

heart to heart

God, I can trust You with my heart!

You are...

I want to tell You about...

Thank You for...

Forgive me for...

God, even when I feel like I can't breathe, breathe Your life and love into me. I know You hold me when I'm crushed. I know You can bring good. Give me courage each day. I know You walk with me.

I am his

he is mine

BUT take heart

I have overcome the WORLD.

John 16:33 ESV

chapter 17

Reflection

1. Who or what is at the center of your world right now? Are you setting yourself on the Rock (Jesus) or setting yourself up for a fall (like in Matthew 7:24-27)?

2. A common struggle is where is God when bad things happen? Recap some things from this chapter. Then read these verses and write down God's promises about going through this world: Psalm 23, Joshua 1:9, Romans 8:28, Isaiah 41:10, 1 Peter 5:7, and John 14:1-3.

3. A twisted and false gospel some may preach is that if you follow Christ everything will be great. But Jesus himself said, "In the world you **will** have tribulation. **But** take heart; I have overcome the world" (John 16:33 ESV). Jesus didn't say it would be easy. He said it would be worth it! How do you see yourself walking with Jesus? Is it worth it? What is your hope in?

4. In looking at Jesus and His disciples' time here on earth–both the amazing days and the difficult ones–what new perspectives do you have about your time here? What do you think about this world not being your real home? Does it excite you, scare you, or make you happy or sad?

5. Read James 1:17. Don't forget about God when things are going great; instead, give God the credit and thanks for the blessings in your life. Creating a habit of giving Him thanks will grow your relationship. What are a couple of your favorite memories or moments that you are thankful for?

heart to heart

Jesus, You have overcome this world!

Help me to take heart in...

Thank you for...

Jesus, You are...

Forgive me for...

This world is temporary and imperfect, but You, Jesus, are faithful and everlasting! Thank You that I don't walk this alone when I walk with You. I want to stay close to You in the good and the bad and trust You will help me through both.

I am his

he is mine

I have finished the race I have kept the faith

2 Timothy 4:7

chapter 18 Reflection

1. Read Ecclesiastes 3:1–13. For everything there is a season. High school was definitely a season for me! What season are you going through right now? What is God teaching you in it? Does knowing that this is only a season give you hope for the future?

2. Read 1 Corinthians 9:24–27. Paul compares life to running a race. What does it take to be a good, long-distance runner? How would this race analogy apply to the things you need to be doing in your life? Paul talks about two different types of rewards–earthly and heavenly. What might these be?

3. A wise person seeks to learn (Proverbs 18:15). Unfortunately, I didn't realize how much of a gift a free education was until I was out of high school. How do you view your education?

4. Read Proverbs 16:3 and Psalm 25:4–10. Have you asked for God's guidance in that next step in your life? Where to go? What classes to take?

5. How do you want to finish strong this year?

heart to heart

God, thank You for walking through each season with me!

This season has been...

I feel...

You are...

Help me...

God, you use each season - the good and the hard. I want to lean on You to finish this season strong in my faith. Thank you that the Holy Spirit can give me strength to do that!

I am his

he is mine

narrow + difficult is the ROAD that leads to life

Matthew 7:13-14

chapter 19 Reflection

1. I heard a pastor once say, "Does your life require a gospel explanation?" What he meant was, do you live in such a way that people wonder why you're different, and the only answer is Jesus?

2. Read Ephesians 6:10–20. What stands out to you when you read about the armor of God? Now read Romans 13:14. One way we can "put on Christ" is by praying the armor over ourselves first thing in the morning as we lean on God to help us stand firm in faith.

3. Would you handle things differently and with greater wisdom if you were more aware of the spiritual battle? For example, if someone is being cruel to you, take a step back. Could he or she be hurting and taking it out on you? Might Satan be attacking the relationship? Does the person even know God? Now, how will you start fighting your battles? Read 2 Chronicles 20, and really dissect all the things they did to fight this battle.

4. Just because you can do something doesn't mean you should. Read Ecclesiastes 10:1–3. How can you tell if you're the fool? How can you keep your heart going in the right direction?

heart to heart

Jesus, focusing on You will lead me on that path to life!

Thank You for...

Steer me away from...

You are...

Forgive me for...

Jesus, this is not going to be easy to go against the norm! I will need You every day to help me stand strong in my faith. Teach me to pray and recognize the spiritual battles around me.

I am his

he is mine

may the genuineness of your

FAITH

though refined

by FIRE

praise, result in

glory & honor

at the revelations

of

JESUS

CHRIST.

1 Peter 1:6-7

chapter

20 Reflection

1. Those who don't know God may test the genuineness of your faith to see if it is real. Your faith is going to be tested. Are you willing to go through the fire if it means God will come out shining more brightly, or will you hide your faith to avoid being persecuted? What is keeping you from shining the hope of Christ? Read Matthew 5:14-16.

2. God has placed you with purpose to show Jesus to those around you. So where are you right now? Make a list of those you need to pray for and "kill with kindness." Share your list with your friends and pray for those on their lists too.

3. It's easy to love on people who are like us. But Jesus reached out to the unpopular, and He loved the unlovable. He even told us to pray for our enemies. Why? Read Luke 5:27-32. Who can you show love to that needs Jesus?

4. "Even if He does not" is a big statement the three men said. Even if God doesn't keep this hard thing from me, even death itself, will I still choose Him? You will be mocked. You will be ridiculed. Today choose who you will bow down to - man or God. Read Joshua 24:14-15 and Galatians 1:10.

heart to heart

God, You are here with me in this!

Thank You that...

I choose...

It's hard to...

Help me...

I want to fix my eyes on Jesus and my promise of Heaven. Until then, strengthen my faith. Even in the hardest of things, You are with me, God. I am not alone! I am not alone!

I am his

he is mine

who can find a
Virtuous
wife?
she is far
more
precious
than
jewels.

Proverbs 31:10

chapter 21

Reflection

1. Were you thinking the same thing I was? That as soon as I listed all the things I wasn't going to do, the good-looking guy would run the other way? But he didn't. What do you think about that? What would that say about the guy if he did run the other way?

2. Which guy do you want to be with–the one who respects and cherishes your God-given standards or the one who wants you to compromise them? What about your friends? Are you hanging out with people who only like you when you're following the crowd, or are you hanging out with friends who like you for who you are and encourage you to stay strong in your faith?

3. So why do you think being the "good girl" is so often made out to be a bad thing in this world? Read John 3:18-21, Romans 13:11-14 and Ephesians 5:1-14. What does the "world" love, and what are we called to be?

4. Read Proverbs 31:10–31. Using your own words, what characteristics stand out to you about this type of woman? Why do you think we rarely see her modeled in media? What kind of woman do you want to be?

5. What's the biggest lesson you learned from this chapter?

heart to heart

God, You have called me out of darkness into light!

Help me shine...

You are...

I'm struggling with...

Thank You for...

Dad, I know You've called me to be different. Sometimes that's hard. Remind me that people need to see the difference so they can see You. Let them see Christ in me and want that.

I am his

he is mine

beware of
false prophets
who
come to you
in SHEEP'S
CLOTHING but
inwardly
are
ravaging
wolves

Matthew 7:15

chapter 22 Reflection

1. What things have you seen or done that you thought were innocent but turned out to be not-so-innocent?

2. Why do you think people in movies seem to be having such a good time with a drink in their hand? Why does Hollywood make you laugh at things that actually go against God's teachings? Why is sex made out to be such a casual thing? What tactics like these have you seen Satan use to make destructive things look innocent?

3. Peer pressure and compromise often starts with one question: What could it hurt? What voice did I rationalize away, and what voices did I listen to instead? Read 1 Peter 5:8-11. What tools have you learned from the Bible so far to help you stand strong?

4. Did you catch me saying that I flirted online with Steven in ways that I wouldn't have in person? What dangers have you noticed with social media? Take a look at some social media tips (pages 127 & 128) and talk about what stands out to you.

5. Look at Matthew 7:15-20 again. What does it mean that you will recognize a wolf in sheep's clothing by "their fruit?" Read Galatians 5:16-25 for the contrast of two kinds of fruit. Then read John 15:5-12. How do we produce good fruit?

heart to heart

God, open my eyes to see the schemes of the enemy.

Thank You for...

Help me with...

You are...

I need to receive Your forgiveness...

God, I don't have to fear because You are with me. Thank You that when I stray, I can come running back to You. Please help me to hear Your voice and choose it over my peers, the world and Satan.

I am his

he is mine

IF you knew the gift of God and who is SAYING to you, "GIVE me A DRINK," you would ask Him and HE would give you living water.

JOHN 4:10

chapter 23

Reflection

1. What stands out to you about the woman at the well in John 4:1-29? What *"well"* do you run to fill what only God can fill? What might come from letting go and letting God take over that area of your life?

2. Do you feel that if you aren't actively pursuing a relationship that you'll miss out? Do you think God needs your help to make it happen? What does God really want from you?

3. Have you had those moments when you feel like, *Who am I that Jesus would even notice me?* How will your life change when you truly embrace who Jesus is and what He is offering you?

4. My journey brought me to a desperate place of seeking more - that's where I found Jesus. So when things don't go your way or you're feeling unsatisfied, ask yourself these questions: How is God pursuing me in this situation? What is He trying to teach me? Is this my chance to really trust God and grow our relationship? What question do you need to ask God right now?

heart to heart

Jesus, I'm letting go and falling into Your loving arms!

I've been trying to fill the hole in my heart with...

You are...

Thank You for...

I need...

Jesus, You have been pursuing me. I want more of You. You alone fill my heart and soul. I love You back.

I am his

he is mine

ephesians 3:20

now to him who is able to do

ABOVE

and

BEYOND

all that we

ASK or THINK

according

to the POWER that

works

in

Us!

chapter 24 Reflection

1. Read Romans 8:28. So if God is working all things for good and for the purpose of bringing people to Him, then are you looking for His work in your everyday life? Don't give things up to coincidence or luck; instead, look for God at work! How have you seen God this week?

2. Read Isaiah 55:8–9. God's ways are not our ways, and God's timing is not our timing; yet, they are both perfect. When my life doesn't quite seem to make sense or go the way I think it should, this helps me to remember God is bigger than what I see. In what situation do you need to remind yourself of these truths?

3. Completely trusting God with my future and heart not only gave me tremendous peace and joy, but it also gave God a freedom to really work for something greater in my life. Read Matthew 6:33 and Proverbs 3:5-6. Could it be that the pieces of the puzzle will fall into the right place as you seek God first and trust Him with your heart? Do you trust Him?

4. How does trying to find your worth or trying to "complete" yourself in a guy or your friends set you up on a shaky foundation? How does finding your worth and yourself complete in Jesus' love change the foundation of your relationships? Read Ephesians 3:16-21.

heart to heart

God, You are bigger than I knew You to be!

Help me trust that You are working in...

Thank You for...

I give You my...

I just want to tell you...

Your ways are higher, God! My vision is limited, but You are working in my life. Help me to start looking for You at work each day. Let me seek You first and trust you with the outcome!

I am his

he is mine

God's love was revealed among us in this way: GOD SENT HIS ONE & ONLY SON into the world so that we might live through HIM.

1 John 4:9

chapter 25 Reflection

1. Do your current relationships reflect Christ? How so, or how not?

2. It's hard to imagine that someone loves you unconditionally, flaws and all, but God does. Read Romans 5:8 and Ephesians 2:8–10. What does God say about His love? Can we lose God's love? Read Romans 8:35–39.

3. God created you, has a plan for you, thinks about you all the time, and is always with you. You were no mistake. Read Psalm 139:13–18. How beautiful does God think you are?

4. Make a list of things you do when you're head-over-heels in love. Have you let yourself completely fall in love with Jesus? What might that look like?

5. What truths have you found from following my search for "the one"? What did I mean by "I found the real thing"?

heart to heart

God, thank You for extending Your love to me by sending Jesus!

Help me to...

You are...

I'm thankful for...

Forgive me for...

Jesus, I don't want to take You for granted anymore. Your love is steadfast and endures even when mine waivers. I hear how much You love me. Help me to believe it and walk daily in that love.

I am his

he is mine

...Perfect love

CASTS

OUT

FEAR

1 John 4:18 ESV

chapter 26

Reflection

1. What kind of foundation do those "try-it-before-you-buy-it" lies set you up for in the future? What's the definition of conditional vs. unconditional love? Read Ephesians 2:4-9 and discuss which love God offers us. Which love do you want your relationships to reflect?

2. My question from the beginning has been: How do you have a lasting relationship? Can you answer that question now? What does a lasting relationship have to be founded on and why?

3. What fears are driving your decisions and may be causing you to miss out on God's best? How can God's perfect love conquer those fears (1 John 4:18)?

4. What did I mean when I said I had to break down the lies of the American Dream? Take a look at what Jesus shares in Matthew 6:19-34. What are some contrasts in a heart's pursuit of Jesus and pursuit of the American Dream? Can you truly pursue both?

5. Read John 14:23. Obedience to God and His Word is an expression of love. As we listen and obey, those lines of communication open up, and God can show us more. As we ignore the things God has already told us, there can be a wedge in our relationship. How have your lines of communication been with God lately? Could there be an area where you're trying to do it your own way instead of God's?

heart to heart

Lord, I can trust You with my future!

I need to give You my fear of...

Help me be obedient in...

Thank you...

You are...

Let my heart's pursuit be You and Your best for me, God. Don't let me settle for the world's way of doing things but turn to Your Word for instruction. Set me back on the right path.

I am his

he is mine

MAKE YOUR WAYS
KNOWN TO ME, LORD;
TEACH ME
YOUR PATHS.
GUIDE ME
IN YOUR TRUTH+TEACH ME,
FOR YOU ARE
the God
of my Salvation;
I WAIT
FOR YOU
ALL DAY LONG.

psalm 25:4-5

chapter 27 Reflection

1. What are you waiting on to fulfill you, and do you believe it can? When I wait on people and things outside of my control, I can feel hopeless. But read in Isaiah 40:31 and notice what happens when we "wait on the Lord" instead. How does this shift of "Who" we wait on change things?

2. Your flesh may be screaming, "Are we there yet?" But it's in the journey itself that the real growth happens. What growth do you hope to see in this season?

3. Like Asaph in Psalm 73:21-25, maybe you're going through a hard season right now, while everyone around you appears to be living it up. How can you avoid grabbing those "pretty packages" of temptation in these waiting seasons when the enemy wants you to settle but Dad is saying, 'No, that's not best.'? What stands out to you when you read that Jesus faced temptation in Matthew 4:1-11?

4. Read the list out loud from page 156 of what God wants for you. Do you trust Him? Are you willing to let God guide you on your journey (not the media, not your peers) to an all-new adventure of living for Him?

5. Read page 158 together and discuss living in God's will for you today! What stands out with where God has you right now?

heart to heart

God, You want the BEST for me!

Let me trust You in...

Forgive me for...

I want...

You are...

Thank You, Dad, that You tell me no even when I pitch a fit. You love me enough to not let me settle. Strengthen me in the waiting, and let me trust You to be my guide.

I am his

he is mine

JESUS

told him, I AM

"the Way

the Truth

and

the Life"

John 14:6

NO ONE COMES to the FATHER

except through Me.

chapter 28

Reflection

1. Read Psalm 37:4. Can you see that our longing for this beautiful story we call a "fairy tale" actually stems from our God-given desire to find our identity and True Love? Discuss how it's Jesus who fulfills every single thing we desire our Prince to be.

2. You've been searching for love, all the while unconditional and unending Love has already been pursuing you! If you haven't already, read Romans 3:23, 6:23, 5:8, 10:13, and 10:9-10. Then read Ephesians 2:4-9. Have you said yes to Jesus and received this gift of grace?

3. Your true identity is found in Jesus, not in your past, not in what you do or in what others say. Have you lost your identity? Who does God say that you are? Read Romans 8:15-17. Find more identity scriptures on page 196 and read them out loud to one another.

4. You were created and called to impact God's kingdom. Read Matthew 28:18-20, John 13:35, Acts 20: 24 and 2 Corinthians 5:17-21. What is our calling, and what is the Good News we are entrusted with? Are you sharing it?

5. Read Revelation 19:6-8. You're a bride of Christ. How does this change how you view your time here on earth as you wait for that "marriage day/ wedding feast" when you will look upon Jesus? Read Matthew 25:1-13. **Are you ready for His return?**

heart to heart

Jesus, You are the only One who saves!

Thank You...

I am...

Forgive me...

I'm in awe of...

Jesus, You have made a way for me! I know I have sinned. I believe You paid it all on the cross and conquered death itself for me. I can only accept this gift of grace You offer me. Jesus, my answer is . . .

I am his

he is mine

I ❤ Jesus

testify Girl

Share How God Spoke to you!

❤❤❤❤

Visit GirlsLiving4God.com/bonuscontent
to share, meet GL4G, and more!

I AM HIS

- A DAUGHTER OF THE KING .... *Romans 8:15-17*
- BEAUTIFUL .... *Psalm 139:14*
- LOVED .... *Ephesians 3:18-19*
- CHOSEN .... *1 Peter 2:9*
- CREATED WITH PURPOSE .... *Ephesians 2:10*
- FORGIVEN .... *1 John 1:9*
- MADE NEW .... *2 Corinthians 5:17*
- MORE THAN A CONQUEROR .... *Romans 8:37-39*
- SET FREE BY JESUS .... *John 8:34-36*
- AN AMBASSADOR OF THE KING .... *2 Corinthians 5:19-21*

HE IS MINE

- MY FATHER .... 1 John 3: 1
- REDEEMER .... Isaiah 43:1
- LOVING .... Romans 5:8
- FAITHFUL .... 2 Timothy 2:13
- NEAR .... Psalm 145 & 34:18
- PROVIDER .... Philippians 4:19
- FULL OF MERCY .... Lamentations 3:22-23
- MY ROCK .... Psalm 62:5-8
- MY PEACE .... Philippians 4:6-7
- LORD OF MY LIFE .... Philippians 2:9-11

GL4G

GIRLS LIVING 4 GOD

Discipling YOU to be strengthened in the Holy Spirit, sharpened in God's Word, and sent out as ambassadors of Jesus Christ.

Through discipleship community, biblically based resources, and Christ-centered events, GL4G hopes to encourage you to:

1. ***SEEK*** God with all you heart (Jer. 29:13)
2. ***TESTIFY*** to His truth (Acts 20:24)
3. Learn to ***FOLLOW*** His voice (John 10:27
4. Be ***COURAGEOUS*** in all you do (Joshua 1:9)

VISIT **WWW.GL4G.COM** TO GET CONNECTED!!

Made in the USA
Columbia, SC
19 November 2024

47061085R00107